To Parents

Thank you for choosing our *Early Learning Fun* as your child's learning companion.

To maximize your child's experience with *Early Learning Fun*, it is vital that you provide a supportive environment in which your child can enjoy doing the activities. Here are some suggestions for you to help your child:

- Children feel a sense of achievement when they try new things and can complete them, so help your child finish whatever tasks he or she starts. Remember to give your child support whenever necessary, but refrain from taking over the task completely.

- Take the time to work with your child. Don't rush them through the activities because children need time to feel engaged with what they are doing.

- Always give encouragement. Positive reinforcement encourages children to learn and sustains their interest in learning. Look for achievements to praise and acknowledge your child's progress whenever possible.

- Nurture your child's creativity. Encourage your child to ask questions, try different ways, and engage him or her in spin-off activities that you may come up with.

With your involvement and encouragement, we are sure that your child will find working through *Early Learning Fun* a fun and rewarding experience.

Contents

Preschool Fun

Action Words

Drink	4 – 7
Eat	8 – 11
Jump	12 – 15
Swim	16 – 19
Run	20 – 23

Opposites

Big and Small	24 – 27
Tall and Short	28 – 31
Full and Empty	32 – 35
Hot and Cold	36 – 39

Body Parts

Eye   40 – 43

Ear   44 – 47

Mouth   48 – 51

Nose   52 – 55

Hand   56 – 59

Foot   60 – 63

Drink

Trace the word. Then cut out the pictures and paste them in the correct boxes to see what the children are drinking.

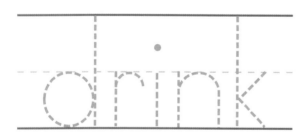

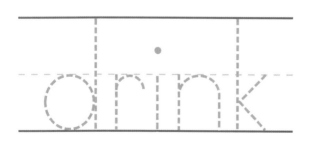

Drink Eat Jump Swim Run

Draw lines from Sally to the containers she can use to drink the juice.

Mrs. Smith is going to give her baby and pets something to drink. Draw lines to pair them up.

Eat

Trace the word. Then color the thing that you can eat.

What do we use to eat these different foods? Cut out the pictures and paste them in the correct boxes.

Drink	**Eat**	Jump	Swim	Run

Put the pictures in order. Write 1 to 4.

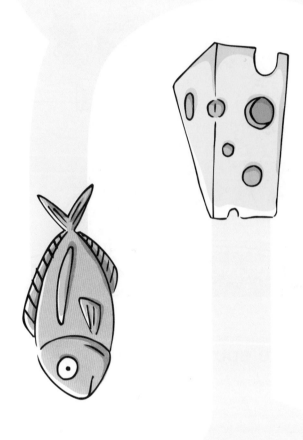

Help the animals find the food that they eat.

Drink	Eat	**Jump**	Swim	Run

Jump

Trace the word. Then color the spot that the boy will jump into.

jump

jump

Trace the lines to show how the frog jumps to the fly.

Drink   Eat   **Jump**   Swim   Run

Draw a path to show how Sally jumps to the finish line.

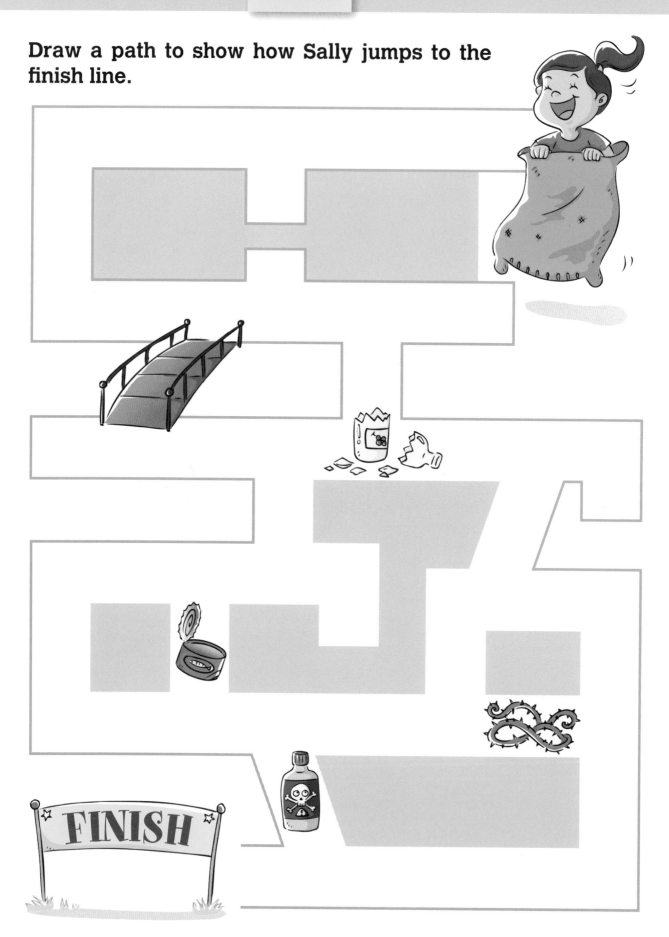

Color the animals that can jump. Then draw a line to show how each of them jumps.

Swim

Trace the word. Then color the animals that can swim.

swim

swim

Draw lines to show Melissa where she can swim.

Color the things that are used for swimming.

Trace the wavy lines. Then color the swimming fish in the sea.

Run

Trace the word. Then color the boy who is running.

Trace the lines to show how much farther each child has to run. Then color the child who will win.

Simon is going to run a race. Color the clothes and shoes that he should wear.

Color the animals that can run.

Big   Tall   Full   Hot

Big and Small

Trace the words. Then color the big flower red and the small one yellow.

Trace the big and small circles. Then color the mushrooms.

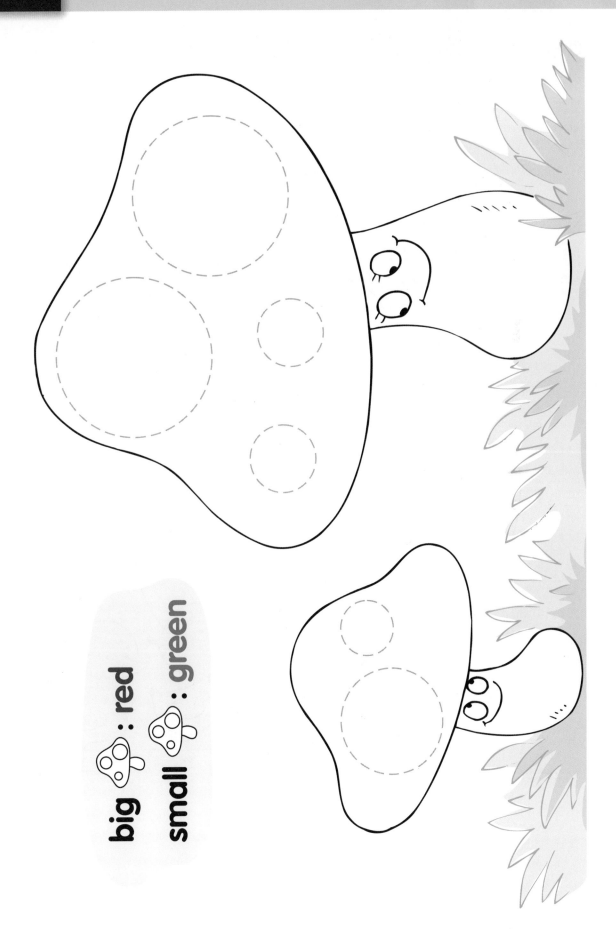

big 🍄 : red

small 🍄 : green

Big	Tall	Full	Hot

Color the picture. Then write "big" or "small" in each box.

Draw lines to give each mouse the right amount of food.

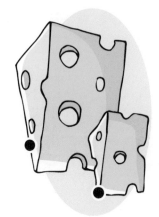

Big	**Tall**	Full	Hot

Tall and Short

Trace the words and the tall building. Then color the buildings.

Cut out the pictures and paste them in the correct boxes. Then color the correct robot that matches the word.

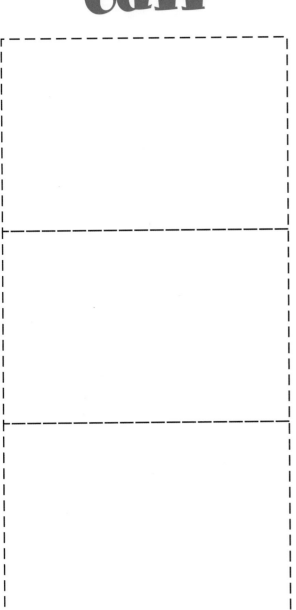

Opposites

Big

Trace the word. Then color the objects that match the word.

| Big | Tall | **Full** | Hot |

Full and Empty

Trace the words. Then match the pictures with the words.

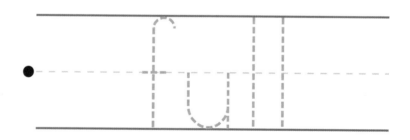

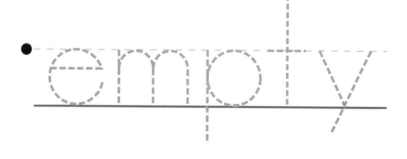

Trace the words. Then do the matching.

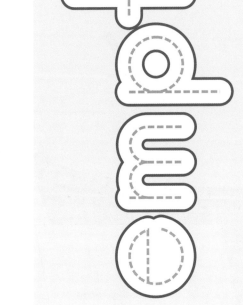

Trace the dotted lines to bring the fruits to the basket. Then draw the fruits in the basket to make it full.

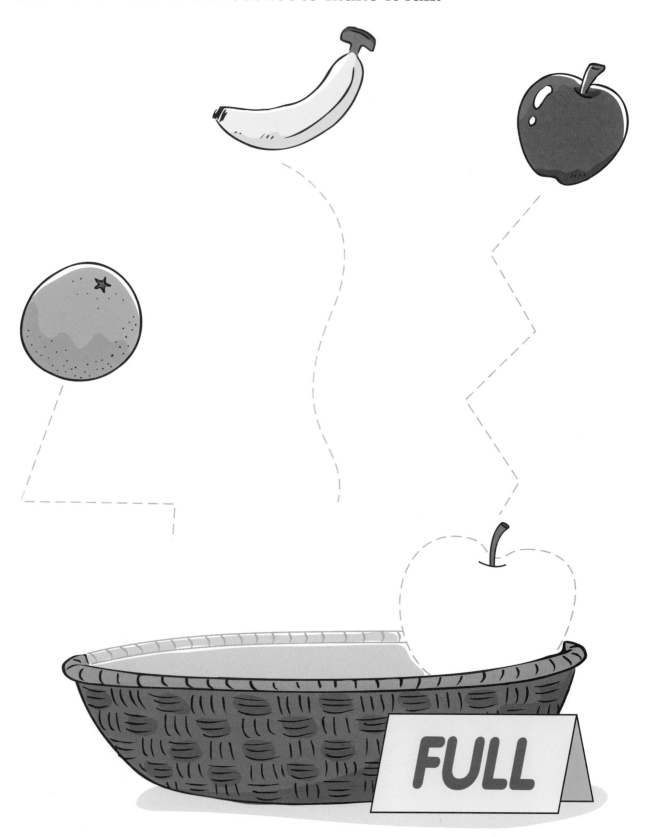

Color each full/empty pair with the same color.

| Big | Tall | Full | **Hot** |

Hot and Cold

Trace the words. Then color the drink that the boy needs.

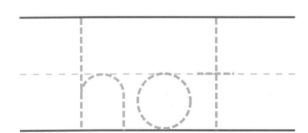

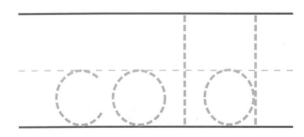

Color the items. Then cut out the word that describes them and paste it in the box.

Big   Tall   Full   **Hot**

Trace the word. Then match the word with the things that are hot.

Color the food items.

hot:

cold:

Eye Ear Mouth Nose Hand Foot

Eye

Trace the word. Circle the pair of eyes that you like.

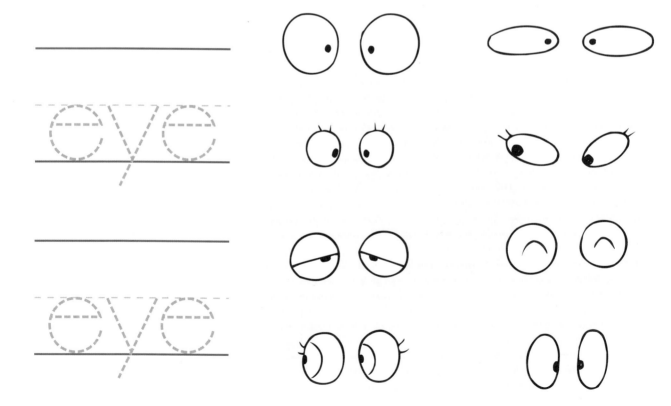

Draw the eyes of each animal. Then color the animals.

What can you see with your eyes? Draw
lines from the pictures to the girl.

I can see...

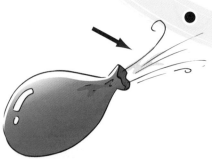

Draw a line to show which tool each boy needs.

Ear

Trace the word. Cut out the ears of the animals and paste them in the correct boxes.

ear

ear

Eye | **Ear** | Mouth | Nose | Hand | Foot

Color the things that we use with our ears.

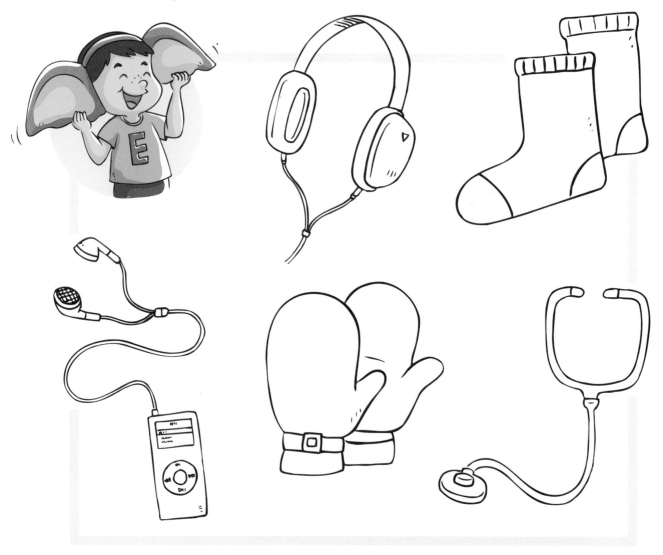

Draw lines to match the ears with the correct animals.

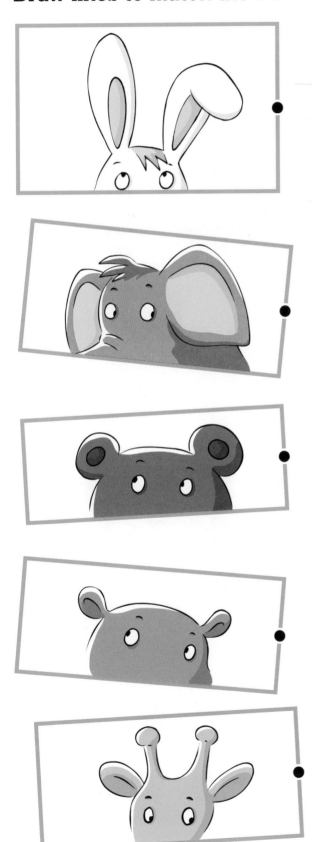

Mouth

Trace the word. Draw the mouth to complete the picture.

mouth

mouth

Choose the mouth that you like. Cut it out and paste it on the clown. Then color the clown.

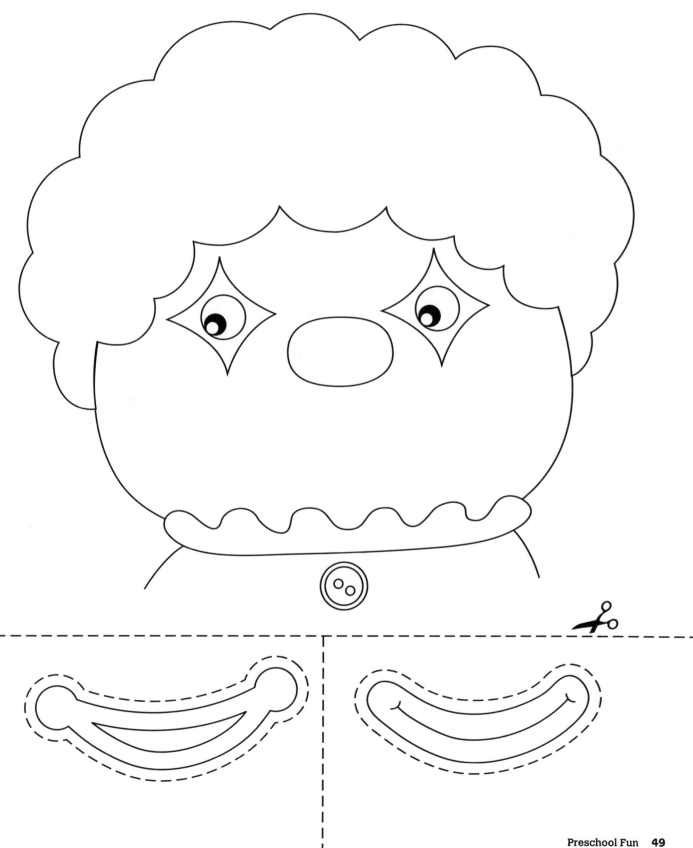

Draw lines to match the mouths with the correct animals.

Circle the children who are doing the tasks with their mouths.

Nose

Trace the word. Color the nose.

nose

nose

Cut out the pieces and paste them in the correct spaces to complete the puzzle.

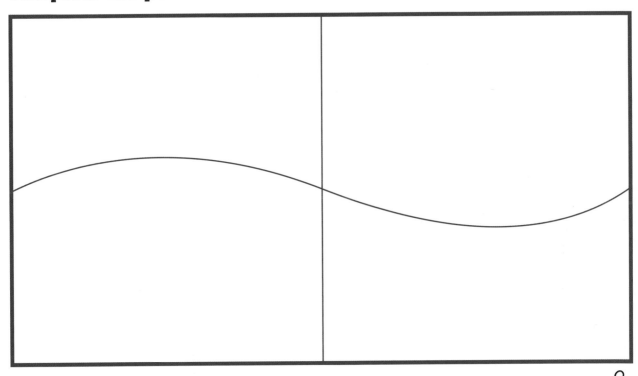

breathe   smell

Help each animal find the picture of its nose.

Hand

Trace the word and the handprint.

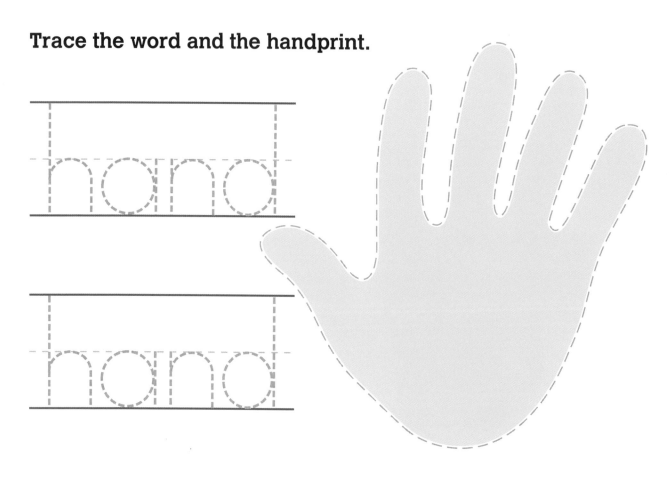

Count the number of fingers that are up. Match them with the correct numbers.

- 1
- 2
- 3
- 4
- 5

Color the items that protect your hands.

Outline your hand. Then color it.

My Hand

Foot

Trace the word. Color the foot lollipop.

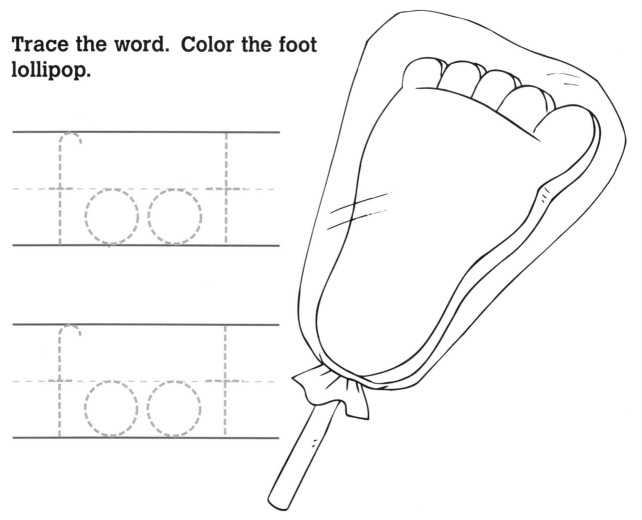

Cut out the footwear and paste it in the correct box to match with each set of clothes.

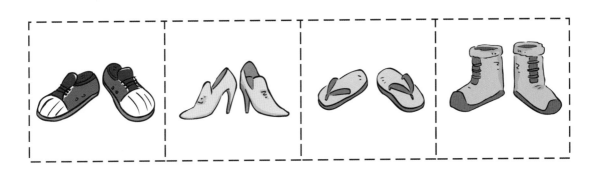

Trace the footprints. Then color each footprint to match with the one that belongs to each animal.

Color the footprints to take the boy to the beach.